The Nature Kid's Guide to
CASSOWARIES

DAVID ANDERSON

For information address LP Media Inc. Publishing,
30012 Variolite St NW, Princeton MN 55371
www.lpmedia.org

Publication Data

Cassowaries
The Nature Kid's Guide to Cassowaries — First edition.

Summary: "Learn all about Cassowaries, the Nature Kid Way"
— Provided by publisher.

ISBN: 979-8-89818-223-6

[1. Cassowaries – Non-Fiction] I. Title.

Title: The Nature Kid's Guide to Cassowaries

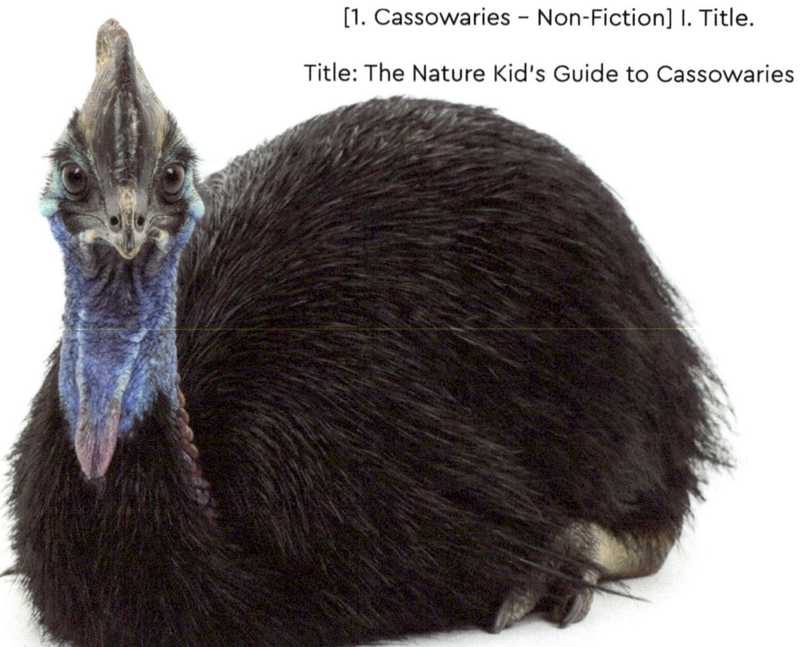

CONTENTS

JUNGLE GIANTS

Rustle! A huge bird pushes through the thick jungle.

Cassowaries are big birds that live in rainforests. They have shiny black feathers and bright blue skin on their necks. These tall birds cannot fly.

The forest floor is their home. They walk through thick trees and tall ferns. Wet leaves and ripe fruit cover the ground all around them.

Rain falls a lot in their jungle home. The warm, wet forest gives them food and shade. Without these jungles, cassowaries could not survive.

HOME TURF

FUN FACT!
New Guinea is the second biggest island on Earth — and cassowaries have lived there for millions of years!

Crunch! A cassowary steps on leaves in a faraway land.

Cassowaries live in hot, green lands. In the northern part of Australia you can find the Southern Cassowary. You can also find it in New Guinea along with the Northern Cassowary and the Dwarf Cassowary. Some also live on small islands nearby.

Each kind of cassowary has its own range. The southern cassowary lives in the wettest forests. The dwarf cassowary prefers hilly land higher up in the mountains.

These birds stay in the same area for years. They know exactly where to find the best food. A single bird's home range can cover miles of forest.

SIZING UP

Female cassowaries are always bigger than males — sometimes by 20 pounds or more!

Thump, thump, thump! A heavy cassowary stomps down the trail.

A southern cassowary can stand 6 feet tall. That is as tall as a grown-up! It is one of the biggest birds alive today.

This bird can weigh over 130 pounds. Only ostriches and emus are bigger. Those powerful legs carry a lot of weight.

The dwarf cassowary is the smallest kind. It stands about 3 feet tall — roughly the height of a five-year-old kid. But even the small ones are surprisingly strong.

COOL CASQUES

Scratch! A cassowary rubs its beak against a low branch.

Every cassowary has a hard bump on top of its head. This bump is called a **casque**. It looks like a tough little helmet made of bone.

No one knows for sure what the casque does. Some scientists think it helps the bird push through thick plants. Others believe it keeps the bird cool in hot weather.

The casque grows as the bird gets older. A young bird has a small one. An old bird may have a casque nearly 7 inches tall!

SUPER SENSES

Snap! A cassowary hears a tiny twig break far away.

Cassowaries have amazing hearing. They can hear very low sounds — too low for people to hear at all. This helps them find other birds deep in the forest.

These birds also have sharp eyes. They can spot ripe fruit on the shadowy ground. Good eyesight helps them stay safe from danger, too.

A cassowary's sense of smell is strong as well. It can sniff out fruit hidden under piles of leaves. All three senses work together to help this bird survive.

KILLER KICKS

Cassowaries have been called the most dangerous birds in the world because of their deadly kicks!

Slash! A cassowary swings its sharp claw through the air.

Cassowaries have powerful legs and razor-sharp claws. The inner claw on each foot can grow 5 inches long — like a dagger! One kick can hurt even a large animal.

When a cassowary feels trapped, it kicks hard. It leaps up and strikes with both feet at once. Most animals quickly learn to stay away.

These birds do not look for fights. They would rather run or hide. But if they must, they can defend themselves fiercely.

FRUIT FEAST
DID YOU KNOW?
Cassowaries eat over 200 different kinds of rainforest fruits — some that no other animal can digest!
16

Munch! A cassowary grabs a big berry from the forest floor.

Cassowaries love fruit more than any other food. They eat berries, figs, and plums that fall to the ground. Some fruits they eat are as big as apples!

These birds swallow fruit whole. The seeds come out later in their droppings, often far from the parent tree. This spreads seeds all over the forest and helps new trees grow.

Cassowaries also eat snails, bugs, and small animals. But fruit is always their top pick. One hungry bird can gobble up 11 pounds of fruit in a single day.

BOOM TALK

Baby cassowaries make soft peeping sounds to talk to their dad — totally different from the adult's thundering boom!

Boom! A deep sound rolls through the trees like thunder.

Cassowaries make the deepest sound of any bird. The boom is so low that you feel it more than hear it. It travels far through the thick forest.

These birds also hiss, grunt, and rumble. A cassowary may boom to find a **mate** or warn others away. Each sound means something different.

Cassowaries do not sing like songbirds. Instead, they use these deep calls to communicate. It is their own special way to stay in touch across the jungle.

SNEAKY STALKERS
DID YOU KNOW?
Wild pigs can be egg thieves — they dig up cassowary nests and gobble the eggs whole!

Growl! A cassowary spots a wild dog creeping through the brush.

Adult cassowaries do not have many predators. They are simply too big and strong for most animals to attack. But some creatures still try.

Wild dogs called dingoes can be a danger. Crocodiles sometimes attack near rivers. Large pythons may also hunt young birds when they get the chance.

Baby cassowaries face more threats than adults. Small chicks can be grabbed by monitor lizards or large hawks. That is why they need their father nearby to protect them.

RUN FAST

FUN
FACT!
A frightened cassowary can leap over a fence nearly 5 feet tall — from a standing start!

Whoosh! A cassowary dashes away from danger in a flash.

A cassowary's best escape plan is to run. When scared, it bolts into the thick forest. Its dark feathers help it vanish into the shadows.

This bird can crash through dense brush without slowing down. It tucks its head low and charges forward like a battering ram. Branches slide right off its tough, glossy feathers.

If running does not work, a cassowary stands tall. It puffs up its body to look even bigger and more dangerous. This display often scares other animals away.

SPEED DEMONS

Zoom! A cassowary races through the trees at top speed.

A cassowary can run up to 31 miles per hour. That is faster than you can ride your bike! Strong, muscular legs give them explosive power.

These birds are also surprisingly good swimmers. They can cross wide rivers and even paddle through ocean waves. Big feet help them push through the water.

Most of the time, cassowaries walk slowly. They stroll through the forest searching for food. But when they need speed, watch out!

DAY LIFE

Cassowaries love to bathe! They splash in streams and puddles to cool off and clean their feathers.

Plunk! A cassowary plucks a berry from the forest floor.

Cassowaries spend most of their day looking for food. They walk slowly through the forest in the cool morning hours. When the day gets hot, they rest in shady spots.

These birds like to follow the same paths each day. They check their favorite fruit trees one by one, like visiting old friends. If a tree has ripe fruit, they stop for a long snack.

At night, cassowaries find a safe place to sleep. They sit down on the ground and tuck in their legs. The dark forest hides them until morning.

LONE BIRDS
FUN FACT!
When two cassowaries meet at a fruit tree, the bigger one always eats first — no arguments!
28

Hush! A single cassowary slips through the quiet forest.

Cassowaries are **solitary** birds. That means they like to live alone. You will almost never see two adults together.

Each bird has its own part of the forest. It does not share its food or space with others. If two cassowaries meet, they may hiss, grunt, or chase each other away.

The only time these birds come together is to mate. After that, they go their separate ways again. Living alone helps each bird find enough food to survive.

DANCE
DATES

FUN
FACT!
A female cassowary may mate with several different males each year — leaving each one with eggs to raise!

Thrum! A female cassowary booms loudly to call a mate.

When it is time to mate, the female cassowary searches for a male. She walks up to him and puffs out her bright blue neck. Her colors seem to glow in the dim forest light.

The two birds circle each other slowly. The male makes soft sounds and bobs his head up and down. If the female likes him, she stays close.

After they mate, the female walks away. She leaves the male to care for the eggs all by himself. Then she goes off to find another mate.

CUTE CHICKS

DID YOU KNOW?
Baby cassowaries can walk and find food on their own within just a few days of hatching!

Crack! A baby cassowary walks the jungle floor for the first time.

Cassowary eggs are green and very big — about the size of a grapefruit. A female lays three to five eggs at once. It takes about 50 days for them to hatch.

Baby cassowaries have light brown and cream stripes. These stripes help them hide among the leafy forest floor. They look completely different from their dark parents.

As the chicks grow, their stripes slowly fade. They turn brown, then gradually become glossy black. It takes about three years to look like a full adult.

SUPER DADS

DID YOU KNOW?
A father cassowary may lose one-third of his body weight while sitting on eggs!

Poof! The mother slips away and leaves the nest behind.

The father cassowary does all the hard work. He sits on the eggs to keep them warm and growing. He barely eats or drinks for nearly two months until they hatch!

Once the chicks hatch, the father leads them through the forest. He shows them which fruits are safe to eat and keeps them warm at night. He is teacher and protector all in one.

The dad guards his chicks for up to nine months. He chases away any animal that gets too close. Cassowary dads are some of the best bird fathers in the world.

LOSING HOMES

The southern cassowary is listed as endangered in Australia — every single bird matters!

Crash! Trees fall as machines clear the cassowary's forest.

Cassowaries are in trouble. People cut down forests to build roads and homes. When trees disappear, cassowaries lose their food and shelter.

Cars are also a big danger. Many cassowaries are hit while crossing roads near forests. Dogs that live with people sometimes chase and attack them, too.

Storms and floods can destroy nests and fruit trees. All of these problems make life hard for cassowaries. Only about 4,000 are left in Australia today.

HELPING HANDS
FUN FACT!
Some Australian towns put up bright yellow cassowary crossing signs — drivers slow down to let the big birds pass!
NEXT 2 km

Click! A ranger snaps a photo of a cassowary in the wild.

People are working hard to save cassowaries. Rangers guard their forests and keep them safe from harm. Scientists study the birds to learn what they need to survive.

Conservation groups plant trees to rebuild lost **habitat**. They create safe wildlife **corridors** so cassowaries can move between forests. Every new tree helps.

Kids can help, too! Learning about cassowaries is a great start. Telling friends and family spreads the word. Together, we can keep these amazing jungle giants alive for generations to come.

GLOSSARY

casque

The hard bump on top of
a cassowary's head

solitary

Preferring to live alone
rather than in groups

habitat

The natural home of an
animal or plant

mate

To come together to have
babies

corridor

A strip of wild land that
connects two areas so
animals can travel safely
between them